Psalm 119

in Twenty-Two Days

Bible Commentary

Andrew Wommack

Published in partnership between Andrew Wommack Ministries and Harrison House Publishers.
Woodland Park, CO 80863–Shippensburg, PA 17257

ISBN 13 TP: 978-1-59548-729-2

For Worldwide Distribution, Printed in the USA

1 2 3 4 5 6 / 27 26 25 24

Contents

Introduction

Psalm 119 is not only the longest psalm in the Bible; it is unique. There are twenty-two letters of the Hebrew alphabet which begin twenty-two segments of eight verses each. It also refers to God's Word in some way in each of the 176 verses.

This psalm is all about the importance of God's Word.

I encourage you to read one segment of verses every day for twenty-two days. Also, take the time to read the comments on each verse and look up all the references in my notes. In a little over three weeks, you will look up over 400 other verses and be referred to thirty-six of my *Living Commentary* footnotes from all over the Bible.

I believe these twenty-two days could forever change you for the better. I guarantee you will come away with a greater appreciation for the Word of God and what it will do in your life.

Get ready to have God's Word cleanse your heart (Ps. 119:9), keep you from sin (Ps. 119:11), make you come alive (Ps. 119:25), make you have more understanding than most (Ps. 119:99–100 and 130), and give you so much peace that nothing will offend you (Ps. 119:165).

This is just a small list of what God promises in this psalm. I pray you discover and experience all the benefits of putting God's Word first place in your life.

א Aleph

Psalm 119:1

Blessed are *the undefiled in the way, who walk in the law of the Lord.*

The *New International Version* has a note at this first verse which says, "This psalm is an acrostic poem; the verses of each stanza begin with the same letter of the Hebrew alphabet."[1] Each verse of this psalm mentions God's Word in some fashion.

Psalm 119:2

Blessed are *they that keep his testimonies, and* that *seek him with the whole heart.*

God's divine favor is on those who keep His Word and seek Him with their whole hearts (see my note at Jeremiah 29:13).[2] Indeed, there is no way to seek God with our whole hearts without keeping His Word. They go hand in hand. Those who say they are seeking God yet have no love for or desire to follow the instructions of God's Word are liars (1 John 2:4).

Psalm 119:3

They also do no iniquity: they walk in his ways.

Seeking the Lord yields the good fruit of right living.

Psalm 119:4

Thou hast commanded us to keep thy precepts diligently.

Keeping the Lord's precepts is not a suggestion. It's a command (John 14:15).

Psalm 119:5

O that my ways were directed to keep thy statutes!

The New Testament believer's ways are directed to keep God's Word (Jer. 31:31–35). The sinful nature that compelled us to sin has been crucified with Jesus (see my notes at Romans 6:5–6).[3] Now all that's required for us to keep His Word is the renewing of our minds (Rom. 12:2).

Psalm 119:6

Then shall I not be ashamed, when I have respect unto all thy commandments.

Notice that this verse does not say we would have no shame when we keep God's Word perfectly. No one can do that (Rom. 3:10–18 and 23). Our flesh fails. Instead, this verse says we will not be ashamed when we have respect for God's Word. To respect God's Word and to keep it are two different things. Jesus is the only one who ever kept God's Word perfectly. We are accepted by our Father (Eph. 1:6) through Jesus' performance for us and our faith in Jesus.

Psalm 119:7

I will praise thee with uprightness of heart, when I shall have learned thy righteous judgments.

Understanding God's Word will enable us to praise God better.

Psalm 119:8

I will keep thy statutes: O forsake me not utterly.

Praise God that in the New Covenant, the Lord will never leave us nor forsake us (Heb. 13:5). We have a better covenant established upon better promises (Heb. 8:6–13), so we don't have to pray like David did here.

ב Beth

Psalm 119:9

Wherewithal shall a young man cleanse his way?
by taking heed thereto *according to thy word.*

This is a powerful passage of Scripture. I remember the Lord speaking this to me early on in my Christian life. I took heed to His Word, and it kept me out of trouble. Thank You, Jesus!

Psalm 119:10

With my whole heart have I sought thee: O let me
not wander from thy commandments.

Seeking God with our whole hearts will lead us to God's Word. There is no way we can truly know God or His ways apart from His Word.

Psalm 119:11

Thy word have I hid in mine heart, that I might not sin against thee.

The Hebrew word that was translated "*hid*" in this verse also means to protect.[4] This is saying that when we put God's Word in our hearts and protect it—keep it from being stolen away (Mark 4:15)—God's Word will keep us from sin. It works.

Psalm 119:12

Blessed art thou, O Lord: teach me thy statutes.

We need the supernatural help of the Lord to understand God's Word. God has promised us that help in the person of the Holy Spirit. There are a number of times in John 14–16 where Jesus said the Holy Spirit was given to teach us all things, to bring us into all truth, and to bring back to our remembrance all the things that Jesus said unto us (John 14:26).

Psalm 119:13

With my lips have I declared all the judgments of thy mouth.

We don't need to keep the truths of God's Word to ourselves. We should speak them out to others.

Psalm 119:14

I have rejoiced in the way of thy testimonies, as much *as in all riches.*

When we rejoice in God's Word more than we rejoice in getting wealthy, then God's Word will release its power in our lives.

Psalm 119:15

I will meditate in thy precepts, and have respect unto thy ways.

There is a difference between meditation and simply reading. It's in meditating on the Word of God that we really reap the benefits of being in God's Word (see my notes on "meditation" at Psalms 1:2 and 2:1).[5]

Psalm 119:16

I will delight myself in thy statutes: I will not forget thy word.

Notice that we have to delight ourselves in God's Word. We can't just ask the Lord to make us like His Word.

We have to choose God's Word. And as we follow through with that commitment, then the delight for God's Word will come.

The Hebrew word *shâkach*, which was translated "*I will not forget*" in this verse, means "to mislay, i.e. to be oblivious of, from want of memory or attention."[6] Those who are ignorant or don't have their memories and attention focused on God's Word have not yet delighted in the statues of God.

ג **Gimel**

Psalm 119:17

Deal bountifully with thy servant, that *I may live, and keep thy word.*

The object of our lives should be to keep God's Word.

Psalm 119:18

Open thou mine eyes, that I may behold wondrous things out of thy law.

We need revelation from the Holy Spirit to really receive the full benefit from God's Word. Here is a scripture we can pray that will grant us that enlightenment. See my note at John 14:26.[7]

The same Hebrew word, pâlâ', that was translated "*wondrous things*" in this verse was translated "*marvellous*" in Psalm 118:23.[8]

Psalm 119:19

I am *a stranger in the earth: hide not thy commandments from me.*

A stranger is a person who is not at home. We don't need to be at home in this world (Heb. 11:8–15).

In other words, we don't know where we are going without God's help. Therefore, Lord, show us Your ways through Your Word.

Psalm 119:20

My soul breaketh for the longing that it hath *unto thy judgments at all times.*

What an awesome statement! If we loved the Word of God this much, we would have the power of God's Word working in us.

Psalm 119:21

Thou hast rebuked the proud that are *cursed,*
which do err from thy commandments.

Proud people don't trust in the Lord; they trust in themselves. Therefore, they aren't dependent on God's Word. They think that they can handle the situation. That kind of thinking leads to destruction (Prov. 16:18).

Notice that the proud are cursed! Anyone who wants to be proud is wanting to be cursed.

First Peter 5:5 says, "*Likewise, ye younger, submit your-selves unto the elder. Yea, all* of you *be subject one to another, and be clothed with humility: for God resisteth the proud, and giveth grace to the humble.*" See also James 4:6.

Psalm 119:22

Remove from me reproach and contempt; for I
have kept thy testimonies.

Keeping God's Word will keep us from reproach (shame and disgrace) and contempt (disrespect). Everyone wants those results, but few will keep God's Word in order to obtain them.

Psalm 119:23

Princes also did sit and *speak against me:* but *thy servant did meditate in thy statutes.*

The antidote to people's criticism is meditating in God's Word. God's Word will show us our acceptance with God (Eph. 1:6). When we are thinking on how God loves and accepts us; we won't care what men have to say. Those who are moved by the rejection of men are not basking in the acceptance of their heavenly Father.

Psalm 119:24

Thy testimonies also are *my delight* and *my counsellers.*

The counsel of God's Word is better than the counsel of the wisest men.

ᴛ Daleth

Psalm 119:25

My soul cleaveth unto the dust: quicken thou me according to thy word.

In other words, our souls tend toward death. But God's Word will make us come alive to righteousness. The entrance of God's Word brings light and gives understanding to the simple (Ps. 119:130).

Psalm 119:26

I have declared my ways, and thou heardest me:
teach me thy statutes.

The Holy Spirit is given to the New Testament believer to teach us (John 14:26).

Psalm 119:27

Make me to understand the way of thy precepts: so
shall I talk of thy wondrous works.

We can't truly instruct others in the ways of God until we understand God's ways through His Word (Ps. 119:18).

Psalm 119:28

My soul melteth for heaviness: strengthen thou me
according unto thy word.

The word "*heaviness*" is referring to sorrow or grief. The *New International Version* says, "*My soul is weary with sorrow; strengthen me according to your word.*" God's Word will make us strong emotionally (Ps. 19:8).

Psalm 119:29

Remove from me the way of lying: and grant me thy law graciously.

Satan is the father of all lies (John 8:44), and God is the Father of all truth (Heb. 6:17–18). God's Word will cause us to walk in truth (John 17:17) and turn us from lying.

Psalm 119:30

I have chosen the way of truth: thy judgments have I laid before me.

No one can claim to be committed to the truth without being committed to God's Word. God's Word is truth (John 17:17).

Psalm 119:31

I have stuck unto thy testimonies: O Lord, put me not to shame.

The Hebrew word that is translated "*stuck*" in this verse means, "properly, to impinge, i.e. cling or adhere;

figuratively, to catch by pursuit."[9] This is reflected in the *Amplified Bible* translation which says, "*I cling tightly to Your testimonies; O Lord, do not put me to shame!*"

Psalm 119:32

*I will run the way of thy commandments, when
thou shalt enlarge my heart.*

Notice the connection between keeping the commandments and having an enlarged ("*willing*" in the *Amplified Bible*) heart.

ה He

Psalm 119:33

*Teach me, O Lord, the way of thy statutes; and I
shall keep it* unto *the end.*

The Bible isn't written to our heads but to our hearts. It takes a heart-level revelation from the Lord to truly know the Word. See my note at Luke 24:45.[10]

Psalm 119:34

Give me understanding, and I shall keep thy law;
yea, I shall observe it with my *whole heart.*

We need to have the quickening power of the Holy Spirit to give us understanding of God's Word (John 14:26). The Bible isn't written to our heads, but rather to our hearts. We can't just figure it out with our peanut brains. We need God's help. See my note at Luke 24:45.[11]

Psalm 119:35

Make me to go in the path of thy commandments;
for therein do I delight.

Psalm 37:4 says, "*Delight thyself also in the Lord; and he shall give thee the desires of thine heart.*" When we choose God's Word by delighting in it, He will put His desires in our hearts.

Psalm 119:36

Incline my heart unto thy testimonies, and not to
covetousness.

The *New International Version* says, "*Turn my heart toward your statutes and not toward selfish gain.*" So, inclining our hearts is speaking of turning, or tuning, our hearts toward God's Word.

Psalm 119:37

Turn away mine eyes from beholding vanity; and *quicken thou me in thy way.*

We should focus on God's Word and not on the vain things that occupy most people. We need God's ability to do this (Phil. 4:13 and 2 Cor. 10:3–5).

Psalm 119:38

Stablish thy word unto thy servant, who is devoted *to thy fear.*

"*Stablish*" simply means "establish."[12] This same Hebrew word was translated "*establish,*" "*established,*" and "*establisheth*" a total of twenty-seven times in the Old Testament.[13]

Psalm 119:39

Turn away my reproach which I fear: for thy judgments are *good.*

Why did the author fear reproach? I'm sure it's because

of something he had done and knew that if it became public knowledge, he would be ruined. Indeed, all of us have sinned and are susceptible to reproach. But the Lord is kind and gracious and will never mention our sins to us again (Heb. 8:12).

Psalm 119:40

Behold, I have longed after thy precepts: quicken me in thy righteousness.

Longing for God's Word quickens us or makes us alive (Heb. 4:12).

ו Vau

Psalm 119:41

Let thy mercies come also unto me, O LORD, even thy salvation, according to thy word.

God is not the problem. He is always looking for ways to get His salvation to us. We are the ones who have to let God's will come to pass in our lives. We have to access His grace through faith (Rom. 5:2).

Psalm 119:42

So shall I have wherewith to answer him that reproacheth me: for I trust in thy word.

Trusting in God's Word will cause us to be able to answer those who reproach us.

Psalm 119:43

And take not the word of truth utterly out of my mouth; for I have hoped in thy judgments.

We don't have to worry about the Lord taking His words of truth out of our mouths. The Lord wants His Word in our mouths more than we do. I suspect this was simply the writer expressing how strong his desire for God's Word was.

Psalm 119:44

So shall I keep thy law continually for ever and ever.

The previous verse (Ps. 119:43) asked the Lord to not take the word of truth out of his mouth. Now this verse links the Word being in our mouth to keeping God's law. This same thing is done in Joshua 1:8. Speaking God's Word is important.

Psalm 119:45

And I will walk at liberty: for I seek thy precepts.

There is no true freedom apart from God's Word (John 8:32, 17:17; and Rom. 8:32–39).

Psalm 119:46

I will speak of thy testimonies also before kings, and will not be ashamed.

We can't be timid about God's Word (Mark 8:38 and Luke 9:26). The fear of man brings a snare (Prov. 29:25) and keeps us from walking in God's faith (John 5:44).

Psalm 119:47

And I will delight myself in thy commandments, which I have loved.

We are to delight in and love God's Word. When we do that, God puts His desires in our hearts (Ps. 37:4).

Psalm 119:48

My hands also will I lift up unto thy commandments, which I have loved; and I will meditate in thy statutes.

Lifting our hands glorifies the Lord (Ps. 134:2). Meditation involves the imagination (see my notes at Psalms 1:2 and 2:1).[14]

ז Zain

Psalm 119:49

Remember the word unto thy servant, upon which thou hast caused me to hope.

God's Word gives us hope (Heb. 6:16–20). Hope is a positive imagination (see my notes at Romans 8:24).[15]

Psalm 119:50

This is *my comfort in my affliction: for thy word hath quickened me.*

"*This*" is referring to hope which was mentioned in the previous verse. There is nothing more comforting than the comfort that the Holy Spirit brings when we are meditating in God's Word (2 Cor. 1:3–4). It literally makes us come alive (Heb. 4:12). Thank You, Jesus!

Psalm 119:51

The proud have had me greatly in derision: yet
have I not declined from thy law.

The root of all strife is pride (see my note at Proverbs
13:10).[16] We cannot let persecution move us off the Word
of God. See my notes at Mark 4:16–17.[17]

Psalm 119:52

*I remembered thy judgments of old, O Lord; and
have comforted myself.*

Remembering God's faithfulness to others brings
comfort to us (Rom. 15:4).

Psalm 119:53

*Horror hath taken hold upon me because of the
wicked that forsake thy law.*

This isn't speaking of horror as we use that word today.
This is speaking of a strong hatred. The *Amplified Bible,
Classic Edition*, says, "*Burning indignation, terror,* and *sad-
ness seize upon me because of the wicked, who forsake Your
law*." Indeed, the fear of the Lord is to hate evil (Prov. 8:13).

Psalm 119:54

Thy statutes have been my songs in the house of my pilgrimage.

The *American Heritage Dictionary* defines "pilgrimage" as "1. A journey to a sacred place or shrine. 2. A long journey or search."[18] We need to be singing as we pass through this life.

Psalm 119:55

I have remembered thy name, O Lord, in the night, and have kept thy law.

Anyone can praise God when the sun is shining and all is right in the world. But the victory comes when we can praise God just as much in the tough night seasons.

Psalm 119:56

This I had, because I kept thy precepts.

Psalm 119:55 speaks of the author praising God through the tough night seasons when things were not all good. Here, this verse says the reason he was able to do that was because he was walking in God's Word. Troubles quickly separate those who are truly committed to God's

Word and those who are not. The difference between con-
sistency and inconsistency is God's Word.

※ ◆ ※

ח Cheth

Psalm 119:57

*Thou art my portion, O Lord: I have said that I
would keep thy words.*

God is our portion. It's not what God can do for us but,
rather, that God Himself is our inheritance (Rom. 8:17).
But when we get God, we get all He is and all He can do
(Rom. 8:32).

Psalm 119:58

*I intreated thy favour with my whole heart: be
merciful unto me according to thy word.*

Everything we have and need is according to God's
Word (see my notes at 2 Peter 1:2–4).[19] We have to seek
the Lord with our whole hearts to obtain (see my note at
Jeremiah 29:13).[20]

Psalm 119:59

I thought on my ways, and turned my feet unto thy testimonies.

If we would honestly consider how we have been running our own lives, we would all turn to God's Word (Jer. 10:23). There is no true, lasting success apart from being led by God. This is why Scripture says to ponder the path of our feet (Prov. 4:26) and to be still and know that He is God (Ps. 46:10).

Psalm 119:60

I made haste, and delayed not to keep thy commandments.

We need to be quick and eager to follow God's Word. It's not good when we turn to the Lord's instructions as a last resort.

Psalm 119:61

The bands of the wicked have robbed me: but *I have not forgotten thy law.*

Even adversity should not turn us from God and His Word. Instead, we should throw ourselves upon God and His mercy even more in times of trouble.

Psalm 119:62

At midnight I will rise to give thanks unto thee
because of thy righteous judgments.

This is describing those who are so committed to and excited about God's Word that they can't sleep without praising God for His Word.

Psalm 119:63

I am a companion of all them that fear thee, and
of them that keep thy precepts.

Our close friends should be those who love and keep God's Word. One of the most important factors in our success is the company we keep (Prov. 13:20, 1 Cor. 15:33, and 2 Cor. 6:14).

Psalm 119:64

The earth, O Lord, is full of thy mercy: teach me
thy statutes.

Psalm 19:1–4 shows that the creation is constantly declaring the glory of God. Those with eyes to see can find the mercy of God in everything He has done.

ט Teth

Psalm 119:65

Thou hast dealt well with thy servant, O Lord,
according unto thy word.

I can certainly say "amen" to that. Really, everyone can. Even if you have been devastated, it's not because of God. The devil is the one who steals, kills, and destroys (John 10:10). The Lord has been more merciful to all of us than any of us deserve (Ezra 9:13).

Psalm 119:66

Teach me good judgment and knowledge: for I
have believed thy commandments.

This is promised to those who receive God's Word (Prov. 2:1–9).

Psalm 119:67

Before I was afflicted I went astray: but now have I
kept thy word.

Suffering often drives people to God's Word for help. But it is not God who brings that suffering (James 1:13–15).

Suffering just comes, primarily from our own self-will. So, God can use suffering, but we need to never blame God for being the source of that suffering.

Psalm 119:68

Thou art *good, and doest good; teach me thy statutes.*

This is a key to understanding God's Word. If we see God as a harsh God and look at the Bible through that filter, we will miss the true nature of God. God is love (1 John 4:8 and 16), and we need to start with that mindset and interpret God's Word in the light of that truth.

Psalm 119:69

The proud have forged a lie against me: but *I will keep thy precepts with* my *whole heart.*

Many people get mad at God when others come out against them unfairly. But God doesn't control those things or the people who do them. It is completely illogical to get mad at God for what people do to us. We should have the attitude spoken of here.

Psalm 119:70

Their heart is as fat as grease; but *I delight in thy law.*

This is speaking of the proud who had lied (Ps. 119:69).

Having your heart fat is a bad thing, as revealed in Isaiah 6:10, Matthew 13:15, and Acts 28:27. It is speaking of being dull and non-receptive to the things of the Lord.

Psalm 119:71

It is *good for me that I have been afflicted; that I might learn thy statutes.*

Just as in Psalm 119:67, God can use suffering or affliction, but we must not credit Him with causing these problems. If we do, that will render us passive toward them. Yet James 4:7 says that we must submit to that which is of God and resist the devil. Resistance and passivity are opposites.

Thinking that God causes our problems for some redemptive work will cause us to yield to them. If we really believe God makes us sick to break us and make us better, then the proper thing to do would be to not take any medicine or go to the doctor. If God is trying to teach us something through sickness, we shouldn't resist. We should learn our lesson. Of course, that is foolish, and so is the idea that God puts problems in our lives to make us better.

We will have problems (John 16:33), and if we learn from those problems, we will be better. But that's not God's system. Second Timothy 3:16–17 says that God's Word will make us perfect and thoroughly furnished unto every good work. We can learn by hard knocks if we don't heed God's Word, but that's not God's will.

Psalm 119:72

The law of thy mouth is *better unto me than thousands of gold and silver.*

Psalm 19:10 says this about God's Word: "*More to be desired* are they *than gold, yea, than much fine gold: sweeter also than honey and the honeycomb.*" This is the same point that was made in Psalm 119:14.

' Jod

Psalm 119:73

Thy hands have made me and fashioned me: give me understanding, that I may learn thy commandments.

God made us and knows exactly how to make us understand His Word. All we need to do is seek (Matt. 7:7–8) and believe that God will reward us with understanding (Heb. 11:6). God wants us to understand His Word more than we want to understand it. We just need to cooperate with Him (see my note at Psalm 119:18).

Psalm 119:74

They that fear thee will be glad when they see me;
because I have hoped in thy word.

People who fear the Lord can recognize others who fear the Lord. God's Word will make noticeable differences in our lives.

Psalm 119:75

I know, O Lord, that thy judgments are *right, and*
that *thou in faithfulness hast afflicted me.*

It was correct for the author to say this as an Old Covenant man. But in the New Covenant, God has placed all our affliction and punishment on Jesus (see my note at John 12:32).[21] Therefore, He will not afflict us, and it would be improper to pray this same prayer. We have a better covenant with better promises (Heb. 8:6).

Psalm 119:76

Let, I pray thee, thy merciful kindness be for my comfort, according to thy word unto thy servant.

The only real comfort in life comes from God. Everyone else and every other thing that we try to comfort ourselves with are only temporary at best. God and His Word are our source for true comfort (2 Cor. 1:3–4).

Psalm 119:77

Let thy tender mercies come unto me, that I may live: for thy law is *my delight.*

God's Word gives us life (Prov. 4:20–22 and Heb. 4:12).

The English word "*delight*" at the end of this verse was translated from the Hebrew word sha'shua' which means "enjoyment."[22]

Psalm 119:78

Let the proud be ashamed; for they dealt perversely with me without a cause: but *I will meditate in thy precepts.*

The best antidote to all the injustices of this life is the Word of God. By meditating on God's Word, we can see that every wrong will be made right and justice will be served. It doesn't always look like that in the natural realm, but a payday is coming where everyone will receive their just rewards. That brings us comfort and keeps us on the right road.

Psalm 119:79

Let those that fear thee turn unto me, and those that have known thy testimonies.

Those who fear God (Prov. 8:13) and keep His Word will be drawn to others who do the same.

Psalm 119:80

Let my heart be sound in thy statutes; that I be not ashamed.

Putting God's Word first place in our lives keeps us from being ashamed. Indeed, everything that causes us shame is a departure from the Word of God.

כ Caph

Psalm 119:81

My soul fainteth for thy salvation: but *I hope in thy word.*

As New Testament believers, our souls don't have to faint waiting for God's salvation. It has already come through Jesus. Now it's a matter of just reaching out and appropriating what God has already done. Thank You, Jesus!

Psalm 119:82

Mine eyes fail for thy word, saying, When wilt thou comfort me?

Thank God that in the New Covenant, God has already comforted us (Gal. 5:22–23). It's all inside, and we have the Holy Spirit to minister that comfort to us (2 Cor. 1:3–4). It's ours for the taking.

Psalm 119:83

For I am become like a bottle in the smoke; yet do I not forget thy statutes.

A bottle in the smoke only gets soot on the outside. The inside won't be touched. Likewise, any contamination for the New Testament believer only takes place in the physical, external realm. Our born-again spirits are perfect (Heb. 12:23) and sealed (Eph. 1:13) until the day of our appearing before the Lord.

Psalm 119:84

How many are *the days of thy servant? when wilt thou execute judgment on them that persecute me?*

The author was saying that he wasn't going to live forever. He needed deliverance right then. Under our New Covenant, we have already received the Atonement (Rom. 5:11). Everything is already ours in Christ. All we need to do is appropriate what has already been provided (see my note at Ephesians 2:8).[23]

Psalm 119:85

The proud have digged pits for me, which are *not after thy law.*

Again, the author was speaking of those who come out against him as "*the proud.*" Proverbs 13:10 says that pride is the only thing that causes strife.

Psalm 119:86

All thy commandments are *faithful: they persecute me wrongfully; help thou me.*

All Scripture is given by the inspiration of God and is faithful (2 Tim. 3:16–17). We can count on every word of it, even down to whether or not words are singular or plural (see my note at Galatians 3:16).[24]

Psalm 119:87

They had almost consumed me upon earth; but I forsook not thy precepts.

We need to stick to God's Word no matter how hard things get in our lives.

Psalm 119:88

Quicken me after thy lovingkindness; so shall I keep the testimony of thy mouth.

It is only through the quickening power of the Holy Spirit that we can keep the Word of God. It can't be done through the power of the flesh. It's only when Christ lives through us (Gal. 2:20).

ל Lamed

Psalm 119:89

For ever, O Lord, thy word is settled in heaven.

God doesn't make mistakes, and He doesn't change His mind. His Word isn't out of date and doesn't need to be revised. It is settled forever. Just like Him, it will never change (Ps. 119:152, 160; Matt. 24:35; and Heb. 13:8).

Psalm 119:90

Thy faithfulness is unto all generations: thou hast established the earth, and it abideth.

Just as God's Word doesn't change (Ps. 119:89), the earth that God's Word created doesn't and won't change until He changes it. Man can't destroy the earth. It's arrogance on our part to think we can. The Lord has told us that He will melt the earth with a fervent heat (2 Pet. 3:10–12) and create a new heaven and a new earth (Rev. 21:1). Until God changes them, they will not be changed. We can rest assured that until the Lord comes again, day and night, summer and winter, seedtime and harvest will not cease (Gen. 8:22). Thank You, Jesus!

Psalm 119:91

They continue this day according to thine
ordinances: for all are *thy servants.*

The world is the way it is today because of God's Word. God spoke the world and the universe into existence (Heb. 11:3), and He holds it all together by the integrity of His Word (Heb. 1:3).

Psalm 119:92

Unless thy law had been *my delights, I should then*
have perished in mine affliction.

God's Word gives us comfort and strength that enables us to bear all things (Ps. 27:13). Those who aren't regularly in God's Word lack that strength. Seven days without God's Word makes one weak.

Psalm 119:93

I will never forget thy precepts: for with them thou
hast quickened me.

The word "quicken" means to make alive. God's Word gives us life (Heb. 4:12). There is no true life apart from the truths of God's Word. If people knew and believed this, they would spend more time meditating in God's Word.

Psalm 119:94

I am thine, save me; for I have sought thy precepts.

The Lord saves those who seek Him with their whole heart (Jer. 29:13).

Psalm 119:95

The wicked have waited for me to destroy me: but
I will consider thy testimonies.

God's Word protects us. Psalm 19:11 says we are warned through God's Word. God's Word makes us wiser than our enemies (Ps. 119:98).

Psalm 119:96

I have seen an end of all perfection: but *thy commandment* is *exceeding broad.*

The only thing perfect in this life is God's Word (Ps. 19:7).

מ **Mem**

Psalm 119:97

O how love I thy law! it is *my meditation all the day.*

This is how all of us should be (Josh. 1:8 and Ps. 1:2). We can meditate on God's Word all day regardless of what our duties and responsibilities are (2 Cor. 10:3–5). It will not hamper our effectiveness but increase it.

Psalm 119:98

Thou through thy commandments hast made me wiser than mine enemies: for they are *ever with me.*

How advantageous is it to be wiser than your enemies! That benefit cannot be calculated. God's Word gives us the edge in every situation. Notice that our enemies are ever with us. We can't avoid confrontation with the enemy (2 Tim. 3:12), but we can win (2 Cor. 2:14 and 1 John 5:4).

Psalm 119:99

I have more understanding than all my teachers: for thy testimonies are *my meditation.*

What a powerful truth. Meditating on God's Word gives us the edge over those who don't do that.

Psalm 119:100

I understand more than the ancients, because I keep thy precepts.

What a wonderful truth. God's Word makes us perfect, thoroughly furnished unto every good work (2 Tim. 3:16). No man who has been thoroughly taught by the Holy Spirit through the Word of God need ever feel inferior to the brightest mind this carnal world has to offer. God's Word doesn't only impart knowledge, it gives understanding.

Psalm 119:101

I have refrained my feet from every evil way, that I might keep thy word.

Meditation in God's Word will cause us to refrain our feet from every evil way (Ps. 119:9–11).

Psalm 119:102

I have not departed from thy judgments: for thou hast taught me.

Anyone who has been taught of the Lord will adhere to God's Word. Therefore, those who don't love and walk in God's Word haven't been taught of the Lord (Ps. 36:1 and 1 John 2:4).

Psalm 119:103

How sweet are thy words unto my taste! yea,
sweeter *than honey to my mouth!*

Psalm 19:10 says, "*More to be desired* are they *than gold, yea, than much fine gold: sweeter also than honey and the honeycomb.*"

Psalm 119:104

*Through thy precepts I get understanding:
therefore I hate every false way.*

Understanding is a major key in the Christian life. Matthew 13:19 reveals that the only type of person who is open prey to the devil is the one who doesn't understand the Word. Therefore, "*Wisdom is the principal thing;* therefore *get wisdom: and with all thy getting get understanding*" (Prov. 4:7). "*The fear of the LORD is to hate evil*" (Prov. 8:13).

נ Nun

Psalm 119:105

Thy word is a lamp unto my feet, and a light unto my path.

Without a lamp or light to show us the way through the darkness of this world, we don't have a chance of not falling flat on our faces. God's Word will illuminate the right way to go and keep us from stepping in the snare of the devil. Those who don't use the light of God's Word are sure to fall prey to the enemy.

Psalm 119:106

I have sworn, and I will perform it, *that I will keep thy righteous judgments.*

We have to commit ourselves to God's Word. The Lord only keeps that which we commit (2 Tim. 1:12). If there is no committing, there is no keeping.

Psalm 119:107

I am afflicted very much: quicken me, O LORD, according unto thy word.

God's Word quickens us, or makes us alive (Ps. 119:25, 88; and Heb. 4:12).

Psalm 119:108

Accept, I beseech thee, the freewill offerings of my mouth, O Lord, and teach me thy judgments.

Our speech will only be acceptable to God when it is controlled by His Word (Ps. 19:14).

Psalm 119:109

My soul is continually in my hand: yet do I not forget thy law.

God gave us the privilege of making our own choices. Our lives are in our hands. But it is only under the direction of God's Holy Spirit that we can ever arrive at the right choices (Jer. 10:23 and Prov. 3:5–6). Therefore, those who are wise will submit their free will to the wisdom of God's Word.

Psalm 119:110

The wicked have laid a snare for me: yet I erred not from thy precepts.

All those who live godly lives will suffer persecution (see my note at 2 Timothy 3:12).[25] But walking in the Word of God will always cause us to triumph (2 Cor. 2:14).

Psalm 119:111

*Thy testimonies have I taken as an heritage for
ever: for they* are *the rejoicing of my heart.*

A heritage is something passed down from preceding generations. The most important thing ever passed down through the years is the written Word of God. If we truly understood how precious God's Word is, then it would be the rejoicing of our hearts.

Psalm 119:112

*I have inclined mine heart to perform thy statutes
alway,* even unto *the end.*

This verse clearly states that the inclination of our hearts is our decision (Deut. 30:19). It takes God's power to bring the right decision to pass; it's not our strength. But the choice to set our hearts upon the things of God puts in motion all the resources of God.

ס **Samech**

Psalm 119:113

I hate vain *thoughts: but thy law do I love.*

The Hebrew word for "vain *thoughts*" here is "*çê'êph*," and it means "divided (in mind)."[26] This verse is contrasting doublemindedness as the opposite of God's Word (James 1:6–8). God's Word is not double-minded. It doesn't flip-flop or contradict itself. It is absolutely reliable in every detail.

Psalm 119:114

Thou art *my hiding place and my shield: I hope in thy word.*

God is our hiding place. When the storms of life are unbearable, all we have to do is stay in Him, safe from the storm. I am in Christ (2 Cor. 5:17), and I'm not coming out.

If hope is a positive imagination (Rom. 8:24), then hoping in God's Word is using our imaginations positively to see the promises of God coming to pass, instead of the negative things coming to pass that our circumstances present.

Psalm 119:115

Depart from me, ye evildoers: for I will keep the commandments of my God.

This is serving notice to all the ungodly that there is nothing they can do to get me out of God's Word.

Psalm 119:116

Uphold me according unto thy word, that I may live: and let me not be ashamed of my hope.

Hope never makes us ashamed (Rom. 5:5). Hope is faith, but it's faith for the future (see my note at Romans 8:24).[27]

Psalm 119:117

Hold thou me up, and I shall be safe: and I will have respect unto thy statutes continually.

Faith in God is the only sure, safe place (Ps. 20:7, 60:11, and 108:12).

Psalm 119:118

Thou hast trodden down all them that err from thy statutes: for their deceit is falsehood.

Any other logic or wisdom that is against the Word of God is wrong (Prov. 21:30) and will be destroyed. The wisdom of this world is foolishness to God (1 Cor. 3:19).

Psalm 119:119

Thou puttest away all the wicked of the earth like *dross: therefore I love thy testimonies.*

See Proverbs 12:7.

Psalm 119:120

My flesh trembleth for fear of thee; and I am afraid of thy judgments.

God's Word is perfect (Ps. 19:7) and powerful. We should reverence God's Word. Those who don't reverence God's Word in this life will have it judge them in the next (John 12:48).

ע Ain

Psalm 119:121

I have done judgment and justice: leave me not to mine oppressors.

When we walk in the light of God's Word, it cleanses us from all sin (John 15:3, 17:17; and 1 John 1:7) and, therefore, delivers us from our oppressors.

Psalm 119:122

Be surety for thy servant for good: let not the proud oppress me.

The word "*surety*" means "3. A pledge…or security. 4. One who has contracted to be responsible for another."[28]

Psalm 119:123

Mine eyes fail for thy salvation, and for the word of thy righteousness.

Just as with Psalm 119:81–82, we don't have to be this way in the New Testament. In the author's time, he was looking forward to the salvation that was yet to come. Therefore, he didn't actually possess it. But we are looking back to the salvation that has already come. We are possessors of what Jesus has already provided. It's a done deal. Therefore, there need not be any longing on our part. Just take advantage of what we already have.

Psalm 119:124

Deal with thy servant according unto thy mercy,
and teach me thy statutes.

Praise God, this is the guaranteed promise to every New Testament believer (John 14:26 and Heb. 8:12).

Psalm 119:125

I am *thy servant; give me understanding, that I*
may know thy testimonies.

Understanding is a gift to be received, not a wage to be earned. If we seek it, we will find it (Matt. 7:7–8). In the New Covenant, we have already been given the mind of Christ (1 Cor. 2:16). We have an unction from the Lord, and we know all things (1 John 2:20). This knowledge is in our spirits, and we have to draw it out (see my notes at 1 Corinthians 14:13–14).[29]

Psalm 119:126

It is time for thee, LORD, *to work: for they have*
made void thy law.

God did work when He sent His Son into this world and broke Satan's dominion and wrought our salvation.

And He will work in the future when Jesus returns and puts down all rule and opposition to His kingdom.

Psalm 119:127

Therefore I love thy commandments above gold;
yea, above fine gold.

Do we love God's Word above much fine gold? We should. Psalm 19:10 says, "*More to be desired* are they *than gold, yea, than much fine gold: sweeter also than honey and the honeycomb*." See Psalm 119:14.

Psalm 119:128

Therefore I esteem all thy *precepts* concerning *all*
things to be *right;* and *I hate every false way.*

God's Word is perfect (Ps. 19:7). It's always right. But it's only when we esteem God's Word as perfect that it begins to work for us (Heb. 4:2). Hating every evil way is part of fearing the Lord (Prov. 8:13).

פ Pe

Psalm 119:129

*Thy testimonies are wonderful: therefore doth my
soul keep them.*

The Hebrew word *pele'* which was translated "*wonder-ful*" in this verse, means "a miracle."[30] God's Word truly is a
miracle in the truths it presents and the way it came to us.

The instructions in God's Word are the greatest set of
principles ever given to mankind. All of man's ways and
ideals pale in comparison. We should keep God's Word just
because it's so wonderful.

Psalm 119:130

*The entrance of thy words giveth light; it giveth
understanding unto the simple.*

Praise the Lord for this verse. God's Word will make
even the most unwise person wise if they will heed the
instruction (Prov. 1:1–6).

The English word "*simple*" is translated from the
Hebrew word *pᵉthîy*, which means "silly (i.e. seducible)."[31]
A person who entertains God's words will not be silly or
seducible.

The *Amplified Bible* translation of this verse says, "*The unfolding of Your [glorious] words give light; Their unfolding gives understanding to the simple (childlike).*" So, this could be denoting those who are uncomplicated or those not being choked by the cares of this world, the deceitfulness of riches, and the lust of other things (Mark 4:19).

Psalm 119:131

I opened my mouth, and panted: for I longed for thy commandments.

This goes along with Psalms 119:20 and 42:1.

Psalm 119:132

Look thou upon me, and be merciful unto me, as thou usest to do unto those that love thy name.

How would we know the great things the Lord has done for those who loved Him in the past if it wasn't for the Word of God? All of those stories were written for our learning and encouragement (1 Cor. 10:6–11). We can count on the Lord to do for us what He did for them if we will just believe as they did. There is no respect of persons with the Lord (Rom. 2:11).

Psalm 119:133

Order my steps in thy word: and let not any iniquity have dominion over me.

God's Word will keep iniquity from having dominion over us (Ps. 119:11). Paul revealed in the New Testament that grace is what breaks the dominion of sin over us (Rom. 6:14).

Psalm 119:134

Deliver me from the oppression of man: so will I keep thy precepts.

1 Timothy 2:1–2 tells us to pray for kings and those in authority over us, that we might lead quiet and peaceable lives in all godliness and honesty. This verse has the same principle. God, grant us the freedom to pursue Your Word.

Psalm 119:135

Make thy face to shine upon thy servant; and teach me thy statutes.

The Lord's face shining upon us is speaking of His favor and blessing being upon us (Num. 6:25; Ps. 80:3, 7, and 19).

Psalm 119:136

Rivers of waters run down mine eyes, because they keep not thy law.

It should grieve us to see rebellion at God's Word.

צ Tzaddi

Psalm 119:137

Righteous art thou, O Lord, and upright are thy judgments.

The *Amplified Bible, Classic Edition,* says, "*[Rigidly] righteous are You, O Lord, and upright are Your judgments* and *all expressions of Your will.*" There aren't strong enough words to convey how righteous God and His judgments are.

Psalm 119:138

Thy testimonies that thou hast commanded are righteous and very faithful.

Every command of God is right because He cannot lie (Heb. 6:18). God is faithful to fulfill every promise He has ever made.

Psalm 119:139

*My zeal hath consumed me, because mine enemies
have forgotten thy words.*

Some people lose hope and zeal when they see the wicked act ungodly. But the psalmist did just the opposite. He was consumed with zeal to fight against the ungodliness. Light always dispels darkness. The darker the world gets, the more we should let our light shine (Matt. 5:14–15).

Psalm 119:140

Thy word is *very pure: therefore thy servant
loveth it.*

What an understatement! God's Word is perfect (Ps. 19:7–9).

Psalm 119:141

I am *small and despised:* yet *do not I forget thy
precepts.*

Praise God that His Word is available to everyone—rich and poor, famous and unknown, the high and mighty and the lowly. Everyone has access to all that is necessary to make one perfect and complete (2 Tim. 3:16–17).

Psalm 119:142

Thy righteousness is an everlasting righteousness,
and thy law is the truth.

John 17:17 says, "*Sanctify them through thy truth: thy word is truth*."

The Lord's standards don't change. Truth is not relative. Truth written in Scripture is still truth today, whether people believe it or not. If they don't believe, they won't receive (Heb. 4:2).

Psalm 119:143

Trouble and anguish have taken hold on me: yet
thy commandments are *my delights.*

Even in (especially in) the midst of trouble, God's word should be our delight.

Psalm 119:144

The righteousness of thy testimonies is *everlasting:*
give me understanding, and I shall live.

This says the righteousness, or correctness (accuracy), of God's Word is eternal. It never goes out of style. It doesn't matter how society changes; God's Word is the same for all generations.

Understanding of God's Word produces life (Prov. 4:20–22).

ק **Koph**

Psalm 119:145

I cried with my whole heart; hear me, O Lord: I will keep thy statutes.

It's only when we seek with our whole heart that we get the proper results (Jer. 29:12–13).

Psalm 119:146

I cried unto thee; save me, and I shall keep thy testimonies.

We need to run to the Lord and not to man for help (Ps. 60:11 and 108:12).

Psalm 119:147

I prevented the dawning of the morning, and cried: I hoped in thy word.

The Amplified Bible, Classic Edition, says, "I anticipated the dawning of the morning and cried [in childlike prayer]; I hoped in Your word." The *New International Version* says, "I rise before dawn and cry for help; I have put my hope in your word."

Psalm 119:148

Mine eyes prevent the night watches, that I might meditate in thy word.

The writer was describing how he looked forward to the night, when he could stay up and meditate on God's Word.

Psalm 119:149

Hear my voice according unto thy lovingkindness: O Lord, quicken me according to thy judgment.

Praise God that in the New Testament we have the promise of 1 John 5:14–15.

Psalm 119:150

They draw nigh that follow after mischief: they are far from thy law.

Following mischief and being far from God's Word go hand in hand. You can't have one without the other.

Psalm 119:151

Thou art near, O Lord; and all thy commandments
are truth.

God is not aloof. He is a very present help in time of trouble (Ps. 46:1). Jesus was called Emmanuel, or God with us (Matt. 1:23). Through the new birth (see my note at John 3:3)[32] God now lives in every true believer (John 14:16–18, Rom. 8:9, 2 Cor. 13:5, and Col. 1:27).

Psalm 119:152

Concerning thy testimonies, I have known of old
that thou hast founded them for ever.

God's Word is never out of date, as many people today view it. Its truths are timeless. It is more up to date than our newspapers or news broadcasts. God's Word will last long after all of its critics are gone.

ר Resh

Psalm 119:153

Consider mine affliction, and deliver me: for I do not forget thy law.

We can be assured that the Lord knows our affliction better than we do. Jesus was tempted in all points like as we are (Heb. 4:15).

Psalm 119:154

Plead my cause, and deliver me: quicken me according to thy word.

The word "*quicken*" means "make alive."[33] See Hebrews 4:12.

Psalm 119:155

Salvation is far from the wicked: for they seek not thy statutes.

God's salvation is linked to His Word. Those who forsake His Word forsake their salvation.

Psalm 119:156

Great are *thy tender mercies, O Lord: quicken me according to thy judgments.*

The English phrase "*thy tender mercies*" here was translated from the Hebrew word *racham*, and this Hebrew word means "compassion (in the plural); by extension, the womb (as cherishing the fetus); by implication, a maiden."[34] The Lord is compassionate and protective of us, like a mother to her child in the womb. And God will never abort us, as some women would their children. We are safe and secure.

Psalm 119:157

Many are *my persecutors and mine enemies;* yet *do I not decline from thy testimonies.*

The purpose of persecution is to steal the Word of God from us. We can't let persecution get us off the track and into the grandstands (see my notes at Mark 4:16–17).[35]

Psalm 119:158

I beheld the transgressors, and was grieved; because they kept not thy word.

Those who love God's Word will be grieved with the ungodliness of the world. We can't love God and the world at the same time (1 John 2:15–16).

Psalm 119:159

Consider how I love thy precepts: quicken me, O Lord, according to thy lovingkindness.

The Lord does consider those who love His Word (Mal. 3:16).

Psalm 119:160

Thy word is true from the beginning: and every one of thy righteous judgments endureth for ever.

God's Word is never out of date. It's totally current in all its judgments and instructions.

ש Schin

Psalm 119:161

Princes have persecuted me without a cause: but my heart standeth in awe of thy word.

We have to focus on God's Word and what He says, not on what people say, even if they are the elite.

Psalm 119:162

I rejoice at thy word, as one that findeth great spoil.

How would you act if you discovered a great treasure? That's the way we should act at the discovery of God's Word. See Psalm 19:7–10.

Psalm 119:163

I hate and abhor lying: but *thy law do I love.*

Those who love God's Word will hate lying (Prov. 8:13). Those who love lying will hate God's Word.

Psalm 119:164

Seven times a day do I praise thee because of thy righteous judgments.

How many of us praise the Lord seven times a day for His perfect Word?

Psalm 119:165

*Great peace have they which love thy law: and
nothing shall offend them.*

Our peace is directly proportional to our love for God's
Word. Isaiah 26:3 says, "*Thou wilt keep* him *in perfect peace*,
whose *mind* is *stayed* on thee: *because he trusteth in thee*."

God's Word is essential for keeping our minds stayed
on God and, therefore, is essential for having peace. Peace
isn't the result of prayer but of meditating on the things of
the Lord (2 Pet. 1:2–4).

This verse says that *nothing* will offend those who love
God's Word.

Psalm 119:166

*Lord, I have hoped for thy salvation, and done thy
commandments.*

It's always good to be doing God's Word, but it's especially good when we are hoping for deliverance. It's insan-
ity to expect salvation and be doing everything contrary to
God's instructions (Rom. 6:16).

Psalm 119:167

My soul hath kept thy testimonies; and I love them exceedingly.

Loving God and His Word will cause right living, not the other way around (see my notes at 1 John 2:4–8).[36]

Psalm 119:168

I have kept thy precepts and thy testimonies: for all my ways are before thee.

If we had a full revelation of God's omnipresence and how that gives Him total knowledge of everything we do (Ps. 139:1–13), we would all keep His commandments.

ת Tau

Psalm 119:169

Let my cry come near before thee, O LORD: give me understanding according to thy word.

Our understanding is "*according to,*" that means "proportional to" or "limited to" God's Word. Understanding comes from God's Word (Ps. 111:10). See Psalm 119:98–99.

Psalm 119:170

Let my supplication come before thee: deliver me according to thy word.

Deliverance comes from God's Word (Ps. 107:20).

Psalm 119:171

My lips shall utter praise, when thou hast taught me thy statutes.

God's Word will cause us to be praisers and not complainers. We need more of God's Word.

Psalm 119:172

My tongue shall speak of thy word: for all thy commandments are *righteousness.*

We not only need our minds stayed on God's Word (Is. 26:3), but we need to be speaking God's Word constantly.

Psalm 119:173

Let thine hand help me; for I have chosen thy precepts.

Choosing God's Word brings His help. God's help is

proportional to our understanding of God's Word (see my note at Psalm 119:169). See 2 Peter 1:3–4.

Psalm 119:174

I have longed for thy salvation, O Lord; and thy law is my delight.

We can't passively seek the Lord. We have to long for His salvation.

The Hebrew word *sha'shua'* which was translated "*delight*" in this verse, means "enjoyment."[37] See my note at Psalm 119:77. See Psalm 37:4.

Psalm 119:175

Let my soul live, and it shall praise thee; and let thy judgments help me.

The result of God's blessing on our life should be us rendering praise back to Him (2 Cor. 9:15).

Psalm 119:176

I have gone astray like a lost sheep; seek thy servant; for I do not forget thy commandments.

This is exactly what Isaiah 53:6 says Jesus did.

Endnotes

1. Holy Bible, New International Version. Grand Rapids, MI: Zondervan, 1978.

2. *Living Commentary* note on Jeremiah 29:13: Many people say that the Lord hasn't answered their prayers. But this verse makes it clear that it's those who seek Him with all their hearts who make a connection with God. Not everyone who calls out to the Lord gets what they want. Sometimes people just want enough help to get out of the mess they are in so they can go right back to living a life of rebellion toward the Lord, but that's not the way it works. Those who seek the Lord with all their hearts will find Him (Matt. 7:7).

3. *Living Commentary* note on Romans 6:5: This verse is not a complete sentence, and therefore, it would be incorrect to base a doctrine on a partial sentence. The next verse clearly states that we have to know some things in order for this resurrection life to manifest in our lives.

   Life for Today Study Bible notes on Romans 6:6: As explained in my note at Romans 6:4, our spirits have already died with Christ unto sin and are already resurrected unto newness of life. Yet this newness of life, which is a reality in our spirits, does not automatically manifest itself in our flesh. This verse makes it very clear that we have to know some things before this resurrection life flows from our spirits into our flesh.

   Facts, whether spiritual or natural, don't govern your life. It's your knowledge or perception of truths that controls your physical emotions and experiences (Prov. 23:7). If someone lied to you about a family member having just died, you would experience sorrow or other negative emotions even though there was no factual basis to feel that way. In the same way, if you were told that a family member had died and it was true, but you didn't believe the report, you would be spared those emotions.

Likewise, we have had the power of sin broken in our lives by our death to sin, and we have the resurrection power of Christ's life in our spirits (see the following note at this verse). But these facts won't change our experiences until we know them and begin to act accordingly. All Christians are already blessed with all spiritual blessings (Eph. 1:3). However, few Christians know that, and even fewer understand it to a degree that it impacts their lives. "*My people are destroyed for lack of knowledge*" (Hos. 4:6).

Walking in resurrection power in our physical lives is dependent on knowing that our "*old man*" (*New International Version: "old self"*) is crucified. If we don't believe that, then there won't be newness of life (Rom. 6:4) or victory for us (see previous note at this verse).

As explained in notes at Romans 6:4, our old selves are already crucified. Yet some people have effectively voided the power of that truth (Mark 7:13) by teaching that we still have an old self, or sin nature, that is constantly being resurrected from the dead. There is no scripture that mentions a daily or even periodical resurrection of our old man. Only Jesus has that power. Satan has no power to accomplish resurrection of any kind.

This common belief that people still have an old man, or sin nature, does not come from Scripture but through observation. People observe a drive to sin, and they assume that it is their old sin nature that drives them to it.

The Scripture does teach that sin produced death (Gen. 2:17; Rom. 5:12, 15, 17, 6:23; and Eph. 2:1), and therefore everyone was born with a spirit that was dead to (or separated from) God. This is the part of people that the Bible calls sin (see note at Romans 5:21), or the "*old man*" (this verse). Therefore, the scriptures do teach that everyone was born with a sin nature, or old man (see note at Romans 7:9). But Paul was making a very clear presentation in these verses that for the Christian, the old self is dead. Christians do not have a nature that is driving them to sin (see note at Rom. 6:2).

If that is so, then why do we seem so bound to sin even after we experience the new birth? The reason is that the old self left behind what this verse calls a "*body*." Just as a person's spirit and soul leave behind a physical body at death, so the old self left behind habits and strongholds in our thoughts and emotions. The reason we as Christians tend to sin is because of unrenewed minds, not because of a sin nature.

God made the mental part of us similar to a computer. We can program our minds so that certain actions and attitudes become automatic. For instance, when we were children, it was a major effort to tie our shoelaces or button our shirts, but as adults, we can now perform those tasks without even thinking about what we are doing. It's like it is just a part of us, but in actuality, it was an acquired trait.

Likewise, our old man ruled our thinking before we were born again. Our old man taught us such things as selfishness, hatred, and fear, as well as placed within us the desire for sin. The old self is now gone, but these negative parts of the old self's body remain. Just as a computer will continue to perform according to its programming until reprogrammed, so our minds continue to lead us on the course that our old man charted until renewed (Rom. 12:2).

Therefore, Christians do not have a part of them that is still of the devil and is driving them to sin. Instead, Christians have been liberated from the part of them that was dead in sin (i.e., the old self; see Ephesians 2:1), and the rest of the Christian life is a renewing of the mind that results in the resurrection life of Jesus being manifest in their physical bodies (2 Cor. 4:11).

Someone might say, "What's the difference? Whether it's my old man or an unrenewed mind, I still struggle with the desire to sin." The difference is enormous! If we still have a sin nature, then we are doomed to lives of schizophrenia (i.e., a split mind), but if it is just our unrenewed minds that cause the problem, then we can see the situation improve as we renew our minds.

If people retained a sin nature even after the new birth, then those who were bound by particular sins before salvation would still be bound by them after salvation. They would just have to refrain from the physical acts, but in their hearts, they would continue to be guilty of committing those sins in thought (see my note at Matt. 5:22). Yet there are millions of examples of people who experience the new birth and are so changed that the very sins that used to enslave them before salvation are now so repulsive to them that they have no desire to commit those acts. They can't even relate to their old selves that did those things, because they are new people (2 Cor. 5:17) with renewed minds.

It is truly liberating to learn that we don't have to commit sins; we choose to do so. Therefore, we can change through the renewing of our minds (Rom. 12:2), because there is no longer a part of us that is a sinner by nature. This is the point that Paul was making in this verse. To experience the resurrection life of Jesus, we have to know that the old self is dead, and then through the renewing of our minds, we destroy the body that the old self left behind, with the end result being that we will not serve sin any longer.

4. *Strong's Definitions*, s.v. "צָפַן" ("tsâphan"), accessed July 23, 2024, https://www.blueletterbible.org/lexicon/h6845/kjv/wlc/0-1/

5. *Living Commentary* note on Psalm 1:2: During David's time, when this was written, the only Word of God the people had was what was called the Law. This was what we now know as the first five books of the Bible (Genesis, Exodus, Leviticus, Numbers, and Deuteronomy). These scriptures were written by Moses and were all the scriptures that existed at that time.

   But now we have the whole canon of Scripture, composing the Word of God. So, for us, David's statement here is not limited to just the first five books of the Bible. David was placing a blessing on those whose delight is in the Word of God and those who meditate in it day and night. This goes along with what David wrote in Psalm 37:4. We could say delighting ourselves in the Law of the Lord is meditating in the Word day and night. Therefore, delighting ourselves in the Lord would be meditating on the Lord day and night (Josh. 1:8). Also, the same Hebrew word that was translated "*meditate*" in this verse was translated "*imagine*" in Psalm 2:1.

   Living Commentary note on Psalm 2:1: The Hebrew word that was translated "*imagine*" in this verse is *hagah*. That's the same word that was translated "meditate" in Psalm 1:2 and "*studieth*" in Proverbs 15:28 and 24:2. This Hebrew word means "to murmur (in pleasure or anger); by implication, to ponder" (*Strong's Definitions*, s.v. "הָגָה" ["hâgâh"], accessed August 5, 2024, https://www.blueletterbible.org/lexicon/h1897/kjv/wlc/0-1/). In the first psalm, David described what the godly meditate on and the results it produces. In this second psalm, he revealed what the heathen meditate on and its disastrous results.

   Since this same Hebrew word was translated "*meditate,*" "imagine," and "*studieth*," it's clear that you cannot meditate or study without your imagination. Meditation is taking words and pondering them until a picture forms in your imagination. Then that picture you see on the inside will dictate what you see on the outside.

The reason the heathen rage is because they don't have the perspective of this psalm. If the ungodly thought about what they were doing in the light of eternity as David described here, they would not do the things they do. The ungodly either are ignorant or choose to ignore the fact that a day of reckoning for their actions is coming.

See these notes on imagination:

- Genesis 6:5; 11:6; 30:37, and 39
- Joshua 1:8
- 1 Chronicles 29:18
- Psalms 2:1; 5:1; 42:5; 103:14; and 143:5
- Proverbs 15:28; 23:7; and 29:18
- Isaiah 26:3
- Matthew 22:37
- Luke 1:51
- Acts 4:25; 16:19; and 27:20
- Romans 1:21; 8:24–25; 15:4, 13, and 29
- 2 Corinthians 10:5
- Ephesians 1:18; 2:3, 12; and 4:18
- 1 Timothy 4:15
- Hebrews 11:1

6. *Strong's Definitions*, s.v. "חָכַשׁ" ("shâkach"), accessed July 23, 2024, https://www.blueletterbible.org/lexicon/h7911/kjv/wlc/0-1/

7. *Living Commentary* note on John 14:26: The Holy Spirit is sent to teach us all things and bring all things to our remembrance that

Jesus has spoken to us. There is no revelation knowledge apart from the enlightening power of the Holy Spirit.

The Holy Spirit is referred to as the "*Comforter*" four times in this discourse from Jesus to His disciples the night before His crucifixion (John 14:16, this verse; 15:26; and 16:7). Also see my note at John 14:17.

Life for Today Study Bible notes on John 14:26: Two of the great differences between the Old Testament saints and the New Testament saints are the indwelling of the Holy Spirit and the quickened understanding that the Holy Spirit gives. Four times in this one discourse, Jesus mentioned the Holy Spirit as being the source of God's revelation (first, this verse; second, John 15:26; third, 16:7–11; and fourth, 16:13–15). See notes at John 16:13.

One of the ministries of the Holy Spirit is to bring back to our remembrance all things that Jesus has spoken unto us. This is the best note-taking system available. Everything that Jesus speaks will be brought back to us, while anything that was from the flesh will not.

This ministry of the Holy Spirit is available to all believers who have received the Holy Spirit, but it is not operable in all Spirit-filled believers. It must be appropriated by faith. With a promise like this, there is no reason for believers to ever confess that they just can't remember the Word of God or the truths it teaches.

8. *Blue Letter Bible*, s.v. "אָלַף" ("pâlâ'"), accessed July 23, 2024, https://www.blueletterbible.org/lexicon/h6381/kjv/wlc/0-2

9. *Strong's Definitions*, s.v. "קָבַד" ("dâbaq"), accessed July 23, 2024, https://www.blueletterbible.org/lexicon/h1692/kjv/wlc/0-1/

10. *Living Commentary* note at Luke 24:45: True understanding of God's Word comes from Him alone. The Word isn't written to our heads; it's written to our hearts. It takes the Holy Spirit to open up our hearts and make the Word of God come alive (John 14:26; 1 John 2:20, and 27). We can't argue anyone into relationship with God. It has to come by revelation (see my notes at Luke 2:26 and John 6:45).

11. See note 9 on Luke 24:45.

12. *American Heritage Dictionary of the English Language*, s.v. "stablish," accessed July 23, 2024, https://ahdictionary.com/word/search.html?q=stablish

13. *Blue Letter Bible*, s.v. "קוּם" ("qûwm"), accessed July 23, 2024, https://www.blueletterbible.org/lexicon/h6965/kjv/wlc/0-1/

14. See note 4 on Psalms 1:2 and 2:1.

15. *Living Commentary* note on Romans 8:24: Paul had been speaking of the glory that is in us (Rom. 8:17) and the day when we would receive glorified bodies and renewed souls that would perfectly manifest that glory. This is the hope to which he was referring. And we can't see the manifestation of that hope as long as we are alive in these bodies. But this is what we are believing for.

Hope is seeing something that can't be seen (see my note at 2 Cor. 4:18). Hope is seeing on the inside what you can't see on the outside. It appears to me that it is a positive imagination.

Imagination is the ability to see things in your heart that you can't see with your eyes, and this is what is being spoken of here. So, I believe you could take all the scriptures on hope and relate them to a positive imagination. See my note on hope at Romans 5:4.

See a list of scriptures on imagination in note 4 on Psalms 1:2 and 2:1.

Life for Today Study Bible note on Romans 8:24: Ephesians 2:8 says, "*For by grace are ye saved through faith.*" Is there a contradiction between these two scriptures? Not at all. Putting faith in God's provision is what saves us, but hope is an important part of faith (see my note at Romans 5:4).

This verse makes it very clear that hope is not based on what is seen. Someone who says "I have no reason to hope" doesn't understand what hope is. Hope comes directly from God (Rom. 15:13) through His Word (Rom. 15:4).

16. *Living Commentary* note on Proverbs 13:10: What an awesome truth! Contention doesn't come because of what others do to us; it's what's inside of us that makes us angry. Therefore, we can't stop our anger by stopping others. We have to go to the root of the problem: our own pride. Pride isn't one cause of contention; this verse says it's the only cause of contention. How can that be?

First, we have to define pride. Pride isn't just arrogance. That's one manifestation of pride. But timidness and shyness are also pride. They are just opposite manifestations of the same root problem. It's like they are opposite ends of the same stick.

Pride, in its simplest terms, is self-centeredness. It doesn't matter if self is focused on how much better than everyone else it is or if it is focused on how much worse than everyone else it is. That's all self-centeredness and pride. Shy people are very self-centered people. They are constantly thinking about what everyone else is thinking of them. That's pride.

Truly humble people are people who are not self-centered. Their estimation of themselves isn't above or below what God says about them. They aren't self-focused. Take Moses for an example. Numbers 12:3 says, "*Now the man Moses was very meek, above all the men which were upon the face of the earth.*" That's quite a statement. And what makes that an even more amazing statement is the fact that Moses wrote that verse.

Religious thinking has taught us that there is no limit to how poorly we can think of ourselves but that the slightest bit of arrogance is pride. But I say that debasing ourselves is pride too. What if Moses hadn't written that he was the meekest person on the face of the earth, because he was worried what people would say about him? Then he wouldn't have been truly meek. True humility is being so God-centered that we literally forget about self. If the Lord tells us to tell others that we are the meekest on the earth, we would do it because we wouldn't think about what repercussions might come our way. If we say "I would never say something like that because of what others would think of me," then we are self-centered or prideful.

It's this pride that makes us angry. If we were dead to ourselves, we wouldn't care what others do to us. A corpse could be insulted, rejected, beaten, or ignored, but that corpse wouldn't respond, because it's dead. The reason we respond so quickly to what others do to us is because we are not dead to ourselves.

It's vain to try to stop our hurt and pain by praying out of our lives every person who rubs us the wrong way. We live in a fallen world. Satan will always have someone who will be more than willing to push our hot buttons. We can't stop that. It's useless to try. But we can deal with our buttons. That button is called pride, or self-centeredness. As we lose ourselves in God, we will become less and less conscious of what others do to us. Only by pride comes contention.

17. *Living Commentary* note on Mark 4:16: The second type of heart condition described in this parable is one where a person understood the Word and was excited about it, but that person didn't take the time to get God's Word rooted inside. Therefore, the Word did germinate, but it couldn't produce fruit because it didn't have a good root system. Roots develop underground, out of sight. Most people want the visible results of fruit, but they don't want to develop the root system necessary to produce and sustain the fruit. A seed that germinates in shallow earth will put all its energies into growth above ground because there is nowhere else for its growth to go. So, at first, it looks better than the seed that is putting its effort into building a good root system. But when the sun starts drying out the plant, the root system isn't there to sustain it, and it will wither and die. Most people don't like the root-building process. They want to experience the benefits of the Word that are visible in their lives, but they don't want to just spend time alone with God in His Word, letting that Word get rooted and established in them. So, there can be visible results in a person's life who only listens to someone else minister the Word. But when things get tough, only the Word that has personal roots in our hearts will bear fruit.

Life for Today Study Bible note on Mark 4:16: The second type of person that Jesus described is one who does receive the Word, even with great joy, but whose commitment to the Word is shallow. Just as a plant must establish a strong root system to sustain its growth, so we must become rooted and grounded in God's Word (Eph. 3:17; Col. 1:23, and 2:7). Too much attention on visible growth will cause us to become impatient and not take the time to become firmly established in the truths of God's Word. This will always result in fruitlessness.

A seed planted in shallow soil will germinate and grow faster than a seed planted in deep soil. The seed in deep soil will put all of its energy toward the roots first, while the seed in shallow soil has no choice but to put its effort into the growth of the plant above the ground. The plant in shallow soil will look like it is far ahead of the other seed for a while, but that will not last. It soon withers and dies, while the seed with roots grows and brings forth fruit.

Likewise, some Christians get very excited over the promises of God's Word but make the mistake of not getting firmly established in those truths before they "jump out on a limb" with them. This kind of people withers away when the heat is on. We can't live off of someone else's commitment to the Word; we must have root in ourselves (Mark 4:17).

Notice that afflictions, persecutions, and tribulations are instruments of the devil and are used to stop God's Word from bearing fruit in our lives. They are not good things that God brings our way to improve us. They are instruments of Satan. These things are designed to take our attention off of God's Word, thereby stopping the Word from taking root in us. It's like the runners who spend all of their time in the grandstands arguing with the hecklers over the way they're running the race. They may win an argument, but they will lose the race. We must not let anything distract us from meditating on God's Word day and night, for then we will make our way prosperous and then we will have good success (Josh. 1:8). By consistently putting God's Word in first place in every area of our lives, we will let that Word become so rooted in us that nothing can get it out.

Living Commentary note on Luke 4:17: Afflictions and persecutions aren't blessings from God. They come against us from the devil in an attempt to steal away the Word of God. Notice that they come for the Word's sake. Persecution isn't personal like we think. It's all about the Word. If you throw a rock into a pack of dogs, the one that yelps the loudest got hit. That's the way it is with persecution. Those who persecute us the most are the ones that are under the most conviction. It really isn't about us but about the conviction of the Holy Spirit, which they are resisting. Look at Saul on the road to Damascus (Acts 9).

18. *American Heritage Dictionary of the English Language*, s.v. "pilgrimage," accessed July 24, 2024, https://ahdictionary.com/word/search.html?q=pilgrimage

19. *Living Commentary* note on 2 Peter 1:2: Most people pray to God to give them peace. But Peter was linking our peace to the knowledge we have.

Imagine trying to pass a car on a hilly or curvy road. You wouldn't have peace as you tried to pass if you didn't know what was around the corner or over the hill. But if you had someone in an aircraft overhead who would tell you what you couldn't see on your own, you could have total peace even though you might be passing on a curve.

Likewise, when we are in communion with the Lord, the knowledge He imparts to us gives us a peace that seems unnatural to those who don't have the benefit of God's perspective. This peace isn't automatic or without effort on our part. If we don't take advantage of God's knowledge, which comes primarily through His Word (2 Pet. 1:4), then this peace won't manifest in our lives.

Notice that grace comes before peace. There isn't any peace if we don't embrace grace (see my note at Romans 5:1). Notice also that grace can be multiplied (James 4:6) according to the knowledge we have.

Living Commentary note on 2 Peter 1:3: Peter was saying that everything we need comes through knowledge. That's because

Jesus has already given us everything we could ever need when we became born again (John 1:16 and Col. 2:9–10). We don't need to get something new; we just need a revelation of what we already have in Christ (Phile. 6). Faith is already present (Gal. 5:22–23). We just need to learn how to use what we have.

Prosperity is already given; we just need to learn the laws that govern God's prosperity and cooperate with them. Healing has already been deposited on the inside of us (1 Pet. 2:24). We have the same power that raised Jesus from the dead (Eph. 1:20). We don't need any more power. We just have to acknowledge what we have (Phile. 6) and learn how to use it.

The *Amplified Bible* translation of this verse says, "*For His divine power has bestowed on us [absolutely] everything necessary for [a dynamic spiritual] life and godliness, through true and personal knowledge of Him who called us by His own glory and excellence.*"

Living Commentary note on 2 Peter 1:4: The knowledge of God (2 Pet. 1:3) has given us all the promises in the Word of God for the purpose of allowing us to partake of God's divine nature. What a deal!

Lust is the inroad of corruption into the world (James 1:14–15). The English word "*lust*" in this verse was translated from the Greek word *epithumia*, and this Greek word means "a longing (especially for what is forbidden)" (*Strong's Definitions*, s.v. "ἐπιθυμία" ["epithymía"], accessed August 7, 2024, https://www.blueletterbible.org/lexicon/g1939/kjv/tr/0-1/).

God's divine nature is already in every true believer (see my note at 2 Corinthians 5:17), but the Word of God is what enables us to partake of it.

20. See note 1 on Jeremiah 29:13.

21. *Living Commentary* note on John 12:32: In the *King James Version*, the word "men" in this verse is italicized, meaning it was added by the translators for clarification but is not in the original text. Therefore, this doesn't necessarily mean Jesus was going to draw all men unto Himself. That is a scriptural truth, but that may not be what this verse is saying.

The subject of John 12:31 is the judgment of this world. Jesus was saying that when He would be crucified, He would draw all of God's judgment upon sin unto Himself. Indeed, He did bear our judgment so that we would never have to be judged. Isaiah prophesied that, through the Messiah, Israel's war with God would be over, for she would receive double for all her sins (see my note at Isaiah 40:2). That didn't happen literally in the nation of Israel, but it did happen literally in the atonement of Christ (2 Cor. 5:21).

John 12:33 would tend to bear out this interpretation that Jesus was drawing all of God's judgment, not men, unto Himself. See my note at that verse.

Life for Today Study Bible note on John 12:32: This verse has been spiritualized to say that as we lift up Jesus through our lives, He will draw all people unto Himself. Although that principle is true, this verse taken in context is talking about the type of death that Jesus would die (John 12:33). The lifting up is speaking of being lifted up from the earth and suspended on a cross in crucifixion. The Jews understood that Jesus was speaking of death (John 12:34).

This is a very clear reference to Jesus being crucified and reveals the extent to which Jesus knew His Father's will. In John 18:32, John says that the reason the Romans were involved in the death of Jesus was because of this prophecy about the method of His execution. Crucifixion was the Roman style of execution.

22. *Strong's Definitions*, s.v. "שַׁעֲשֻׁעַ" ("shaʻshuaʻ"), accessed July 24, 2024, https://www.blueletterbible.org/lexicon/h8191/kjv/wlc/0-1/

23. *Life for Today Study Bible* notes on Ephesians 2:8: Ephesians 2:8–9 states that the basis of our salvation is grace—that is, God's undeserved, unmerited favor toward us as expressed in providing redemption through Christ Jesus. The means of God saving us is through faith. Through faith, we accept God's free gift of salvation that was provided by grace. So, we are saved "*by grace through faith.*"

In previous notes, I have explained that the word "saved" means much more than just forgiveness of sins; it includes healing, prosperity, and deliverance in every area of our lives.

In this verse, the Greek word that was translated "*saved*" is in the perfect tense; this means that something was done and completed in the past yet continues to have present results. God's grace has already provided all spiritual blessings in Christ (Eph. 1:3), and our faith reaches out to God and receives the benefits (Rom. 5:2). The Greek scholar Kenneth S. Wuest translated this verse, "*by grace have you been saved completely in past time, with the present result that you are in a state of salvation which persists through present time*" (Kenneth S. Wuest, *The New Testament; an Expanded Translation* [Grand Rapids: Eerdmans, 1961], 450).

Notice that we are not saved by grace alone. We are saved by grace through faith. Faith grants us admission to God's grace (see note at Romans 5:2). Without faith, God's grace is wasted, and without grace, faith is powerless. Faith in God's grace has to be released to receive what God has provided through Christ (see note at 1 Corinthians 15:10).

God's grace is the same toward everyone. Titus 2:11 says, "*For the grace of God that bringeth salvation hath appeared to all men.*" Therefore, "*all men*" (mankind) have had salvation provided for them (1 John 2:2) and extended toward them by God's grace, but not all are saved. Why? Because not all people have mixed faith with what God has done for them by grace.

Failure to understand the necessity of both grace and faith working together has led to many problems. Some people emphasize God's grace to an extreme that renders faith useless. They say everything is up to God's grace and is controlled sovereignly by Him alone. That's wrong. It's just as wrong to emphasize faith apart from God's grace. That's legalism. Faith doesn't move God. God moves of His own free will by grace, and faith only appropriates what God has already provided through His grace.

Just as sodium and chloride are poisonous by themselves, so grace or faith used independently of each other is deadly. When you mix sodium and chloride together in the proper way, you get salt, which you must have to live. Likewise, putting faith in what God has already provided by grace is the key to victorious Christian living.

———————————

Most people assume the word "*that*" in this verse is referring to our salvation. Our salvation is not of ourselves. It is the gift of God. That is certainly a true statement. However, it is also true that the faith we use for salvation is not of ourselves. It is the gift of God too.

There is a human faith and a supernatural, God-kind of faith. Human faith is based on physical things that we can see, taste, hear, smell, or feel. God's kind of faith believes independently of physical circumstances (see notes at Romans 4:17). To receive God's gift of salvation, we have to use this supernatural, God-kind of faith that isn't limited by our five senses. This is because, to be saved, we must believe for things that we can't see or feel. We haven't seen God or the devil. We haven't seen heaven or hell. Yet, we have to believe that all of these things exist. Human faith can't believe what it can't see.

We are so destitute that we can't even believe the Gospel on our own. To receive God's gift of salvation, we have to receive the supernatural, God-kind of faith first. Where does this faith come from? How do we get it? Romans 10:17 says, "*So then faith cometh by hearing, and hearing by the word of God.*" God's Word contains His faith. As we hear the Word of God about our salvation, God's faith comes so that we can believe the good news of our salvation. We actually use God's faith to get saved.

This God-kind of faith doesn't leave us after the born-again experience. God's faith becomes a fruit of the Spirit that is in our hearts. We never lose this supernatural faith. We just have to renew our minds to the fact that God's faith is in us, and then learn how to use it (see note at Romans 12:3).

———————————

Salvation is described as a gift. The *American Heritage Dictionary* defines "gift" as "something that is bestowed voluntarily and without compensation" (*American Heritage Dictionary of the English Language*, s.v. "gift," accessed August 8, 2024, https://ahdictionary.com/word/search.html?q=gift). See note at Romans 6:23.

When someone gives you a present, you don't ask "How much do I owe you?" Your only response should be "Thank you very much." Many Christians, after receiving the gift of salvation, still think they must work to pay for their acceptance. The only acceptable response to salvation is gratitude and praise to God for His indescribable gift (2 Cor. 9:15). Salvation is a gift to be received (Rom. 6:23), not a wage to be earned.

These verses explain in detail the nature of grace. If it's by grace, then (1) it is not of ourselves (this verse, Rom. 3:28, and Titus 3:5), (2) it is a gift (this verse and Rom. 5:17), (3) it is not of works or human effort (Eph. 2:9, Rom. 11:6, and Titus 3:5), and (4) it excludes man's boasting (Eph. 2:9 and Rom. 3:27).

24. *Life for Today Study Bible* note on Galatians 3:16: Paul had been arguing from Galatians 3:15 that the promise, or covenant, given to Abraham was still in force because no one can add to or take away from a legal covenant. The promise, or covenant, was made with Abraham and his "*seed*" (singular, Gen. 12:2–3, 13:14–15, 15:1, 5–6, 18, 17:2, 7; Rom. 4:6–9, 13–14, 22–25; Gal. 3:14, 22, and 29). The promises were not given to Abraham and his "seeds" (plural, referring to the Jewish people; his descendants) but to his seed, his one descendant, who is Christ. The Greek word for "*seed*" is *sperma*, and it means "'the seed' i.e. the grain or kernel which contains within itself the germ of the future plant" (*Thayer's Greek-English Lexicon*, s.v. "σπέρμα" ["spérma"], accessed August 8, 2024, https://www.blueletterbible.org/lexicon/g4690/kjv/tr/0-1/).

Paul would later argue that believers were the future plants, so to speak, that were in the one seed—Christ. "Thus to Abraham personally and to all those who by faith in Christ are brought into salvation, were the promises made" (Kenneth S. Wuest, *Galatians in the Greek New Testament* [Grand Rapids, MI: Eerdmans, 1944], 101; see also Galatians 3:29). God's promise of justification through faith was given long before the introduction of the Law and always has been the only way to justification with God.

25. *Life for Today Study Bible* notes on 2 Timothy 3:12: The Holy Spirit said through Paul that all who live godly lives suffer persecution. There are no exceptions. This is true in all cultures and with all types of people. The only people who are not persecuted are the ungodly. The only way people will avoid confrontation with the world is if they are headed in the same direction. When they change direction and start swimming upstream, there is resistance. Persecution is not always physical abuse. Criticism, rejection, and other types of reproach are considered persecution as well. These forms of persecution can be some of the deadliest because they are subtle. Many Christians would hold fast to their faith if someone put a gun to their heads and demanded they renounce Christ or else, but some of those same people are fearful of witnessing, because of the rejection they may encounter.

The majority of time that the word "persecution" is used in the New Testament, it was translated from the Greek verb *dioko*, as it was in this case. It means "to pursue (in a hostile manner)... to run after, follow after" (*Thayer's Greek-English Lexicon*, s.v. "διώκω" ["diṓkō"], accessed August 8, 2024, https://www.blueletterbible.org/lexicon/g1377/kjv/tr/0-1/). Persecution is an inevitable part of a true Christian's life. This is a well-established truth in Scripture. Many passages echo this same teaching.

Jesus said, "*The servant is not greater than his lord. If they have persecuted me, they will also persecute you*" (John 15:20). "*But beware of men: for they will deliver you up to the councils, and they will scourge you in their synagogues*" (Matt. 10:17). "*Then shall they deliver you up to be afflicted, and shall kill you: and ye shall be hated of all nations for my name's sake*" (Matt. 24:9). "*But before all these, they shall lay their hands on you, and persecute you, delivering you up to the synagogues, and into prisons, being brought before kings and rulers for my name's sake*" (Luke 21:12). "*They shall put you out of the synagogues: yea, the time cometh, that whosoever killeth you will think that he doeth God service*" (John 16:2). "*Fear none of those things which thou shalt suffer: behold, the devil shall cast some of you into prison, that ye may be tried; and ye shall have tribulation ten days: be thou faithful unto death, and I will give thee a crown of life*" (Rev. 2:10).

Paul said, "*For verily, when we were with you, we told you before that we should suffer tribulation; even as it came to pass, and ye know*" (1 Thess. 3:4). "*And labour, working with our own hands: being reviled, we bless; being persecuted, we suffer it*" (1 Cor. 4:12). Through it all, we must remember that no "*persecution, or famine, or nakedness, or peril, or sword...shall be able to separate us from the love of God, which is in Christ Jesus our Lord*" (Rom. 8:35 and 39).

26. *Strong's Definitions*, s.v. "הֶעֶס" ("çêʻêph"), accessed July 24, 2024, https://www.blueletterbible.org/lexicon/h5588/kjv/wlc/0-1/

27. See note 14 on Romans 8:24.

28. *American Heritage Dictionary of the English Language*, s.v. "surety," accessed July 24, 2024, https://ahdictionary.com/word/search.html?q=surety

29. *Life for Today Study Bible* note on 1 Corinthians 14:13: Given his statement in the previous verse, Paul was encouraging these believers to put ministry to the body ahead of personal ministry. "*He that speaketh in an* unknown *tongue edifieth himself; but he that prophesieth* [see note at 1 Corinthians 14:5] *edifieth the church*" (1 Cor. 14:4, brackets mine). In context, Paul was speaking about interpreting a message in tongues in the church assembly. However, as discussed in my notes at 1 Corinthians 14:2, we can also pray and receive interpretation of our tongues in our private prayer lives too.

    Life for Today Study Bible note on 1 Corinthians 14:14: This is one of the great advantages of speaking in tongues (see note at 1 Corinthians 14:2). Our born-again (see note at John 3:3) spirits are perfect (Heb. 10:10, 14; and 12:23). Our born-again spirits have the mind of Christ (see note at 1 Corinthians 2:16). They have all the power of Christ (Eph. 1:18–20). They are complete (Col. 2:9–10). Therefore, when we are praying from our spirits, we are praying with the mind of Christ, using our most holy faith (Jude 20). Too often, our minds, with all their wrong thinking and unbelief, get in the way. Praying in tongues bypasses our minds and allows our spirits to have unhindered communion with the Father.

30. *Strong's Definitions*, s.v. "אֶלֶף" ("pele'"), accessed July 24, 2024, https://www.blueletterbible.org/lexicon/h6382/kjv/wlc/0-1/

31. *Strong's Definitions*, s.v. "יתְפ" ("pᵉthîy"), accessed July 24, 2024, https://www.blueletterbible.org/lexicon/h6612/kjv/wlc/0-1/

32. *Living Commentary* note on John 3:3: A man or woman without the new birth is spiritually blind. This parallels what Paul said in 1 Corinthians 2:14, "*But the natural man receiveth not the things*

of the Spirit of God: for they are foolishness unto him: neither can he know them, *because they are spiritually discerned.*"

The Greek word anothen, which was translated "again" here, means "from above; by analogy, from the first; by implication, anew" (*Strong's Definitions*, s.v. "ἄνωθεν" ["ánōthen"], accessed July 9, 2024, https://www.blueletterbible.org/lexicon/g509/kjv/tr/0-1/). This is stressing a spiritual birth from above as compared to the physical birth everyone on the earth experiences. See my note on John 3:7.

Life for Today Study Bible notes on John 3:3: The new birth is essential for entering into the kingdom of God (John 3:5). As Jesus explained to Nicodemus, this is not a second physical birth but rather a spiritual birth. Our spiritual man became dead unto (separated from) God through sin (Rom. 3:23, 6:23, 7:9, 11; Eph. 2:1, and 5). Just as we didn't accomplish our physical births, we cannot produce this spiritual rebirth. We are totally incapable of saving ourselves (Jer. 13:23; Rom. 3:10–12, 8:7–8; and Eph. 2:3); therefore, we need a Savior (Titus 1:4; 2:13; 3:4, and 6).

We simply believe on the Lord Jesus Christ, and we are saved (Acts 16:31). Faith is the only condition (Rom. 3:28 and 10:6–9). Faith alone saves; however, saving faith is never alone. As stated in James 2:17–18, "*faith, if it hath not works, is dead, being alone… shew me thy faith without thy works, and I will shew thee my faith by my works.*" Salvation is not a reformation but rather a regeneration, a new birth, a new creation (2 Cor. 5:1), that can only be accomplished by a creative miracle of the Holy Spirit (John 1:13 and 3:5).

Throughout Jesus' earthly ministry, the Jews kept looking for Him to establish a physical kingdom here on the earth and deliver them from the oppression of the Romans (Dan. 7:13–14, 27; Luke 17:20; and Acts 1:6). Although at Jesus' Second Coming, the kingdom of God will physically rule over the nations of the earth (Matt. 25:31–46; Rev. 11:15, and 20:4), Jesus' kingdom is spiritually established by His Word and not carnal weapons (2 Cor. 10:3–5). Jesus said, "*The kingdom of God cometh not with observation...behold, the kingdom of God is within you*" (Luke 17:20–21). Paul said we are already in the kingdom of God (Col. 1:13). The kingdom of God is therefore Christ's "invisible church," His body; it was begun during His earthly ministry and is still ruling the hearts of people today. To be a part of His church (Rom. 12:5 and Eph. 1:22–23), you must be born again.

33. *Holman Bible Dictionary*, s.v. "quick, quicken," accessed July 24, 2024, https://www.studylight.org/dictionaries/eng/hbd/q/quick-quicken.html

34. *Strong's Definitions*, s.v. "רַחַם" (racham), accessed July 24, 2024, https://www.blueletterbible.org/lexicon/h7356/kjv/wlc/0-1/

35. See note 16 on Mark 4:16–17.

36. *Living Commentary* note on John 2:4: Although "*Woman*" was a common way of addressing females of that day, it certainly wasn't an affectionate term you would think a son would employ when speaking to His mother. But Jesus was cutting the "umbilical cord." It was time for Him to be about His true Father's business. She couldn't have claim to Him more than any other woman. Jesus' statement about "*mine hour is not yet come*" reveals at the very least that Jesus was not going to perform this miracle yet and, possibly, that He never intended to meet this need. Jesus said the same thing in John 7:6 and 30.

Life for Today Study Bible note on John 2:4: "*Woman*" was a common way of addressing the females of Jesus' day and was used in the way we would use "Madam." It was not a term of disrespect (compare with Matthew 15:28; John 4:21, 19:26, and 20:15). However, it was not an affectionate or intimate term, as might be expected from a son. Jesus may have addressed her this way to serve as a reminder that He was now operating in His Messianic role and as an ending to His silent submission so that He could be about His Father's business (Luke 2:49–51). His continuing words, "*what have I to do with thee*," must be interpreted as a mild rebuke by any standards. Apparently, Jesus was not disposed, at least not yet, to turn the water into wine, because His hour was not yet come.

Living Commentary note on John 2:5: Even after being mildly rebuked, Mary told the servants to follow Jesus' instructions in anticipation of a remedy to the situation. This is not the intrusion of a mother but the tenacity of faith. This is the key to all miracles. Whatever He says, just do it.

Life for Today Study Bible note on John 2:5: Mary's charge to the servants showed her complete faith in Jesus to do as she asked despite His mild rebuke. This quality of humbleness along with perseverance was also present in the Syrophoenician woman in Mark 7:24–30 whom Jesus said had great faith (Matthew 15:28). Humility is a prerequisite for faith (see notes at Luke 9:46 and John 5:44).

Living Commentary note on John 2:6: A *firkin* equaled about nine gallons. So, each water pot held eighteen to twenty-seven gallons, and all six water pots held 108–162 gallons. The Lord supplied more wine than they could ever use at this feast. This illustrates that He doesn't just barely meet our needs. He is the God of abundance. This also happened with the multiplication of the loaves and fish (Mark 6:40–44). God is El Shaddai, not El Cheapo.

Life for Today Study Bible note on John 2:6: Scholars refer to a *firkin* as being equal to about 9 gallons. That would mean these six water pots full of water turned into between 108 to 162 gallons of wine. This illustrates God's idea of abundance, as does the twelve baskets of fragments left over from feeding the 5,000 men (Matt. 14:15–21, Mark 6:33–44, Luke 9:11–17, and John 6:5–14) and the seven baskets of food remaining after the feeding of the 4,000 men (Matt. 15:32–38 and Mark 8:1–9). Compare with 2 Corinthians 9:8–11.

Living Commentary note on John 2:7: Jesus used the most common of all substances (water) to produce wine. Likewise, He uses the weak, base, and despised things of this world to confound the wise (1 Cor. 1:26–29).

Living Commentary note on John 2:8: If I had been one of these servants, it would have been hard to follow these instructions. The guests were expecting wine, and water would not be welcomed. They either obeyed out of submission to authority or perhaps they had faith in what Jesus could do. Either way, I'm sure they never got over the miracle that was performed right before their eyes.

In a similar way, the Lord calls us to go and give His life to a lost and hurting world. In ourselves, we are like water and unable to meet the need. But when we obey, the Lord turns our inability into just what others need. It's a miracle. Others may credit us, but we know what really happened (John 2:9).

37. See note 21 on "sha'shua'"

Receive Jesus as Your Savior

Choosing to receive Jesus Christ as your Lord and Savior is the most important decision you'll ever make!

God's Word promises, *"That if thou shalt confess with thy mouth the Lord Jesus, and shalt believe in thine heart that God hath raised him from the dead, thou shalt be saved. For with the heart man believeth unto righteousness; and with the mouth confession is made unto salvation"* (Rom. 10:9–10). *"For whosoever shall call upon the name of the Lord shall be saved"* (Rom. 10:13). By His grace, God has already done everything to provide salvation. Your part is simply to believe and receive.

Pray out loud: "Jesus, I acknowledge that I've sinned and need to receive what you did for the forgiveness of my sins. I confess that You are my Lord and Savior. I believe in my heart that God raised You from the dead. By faith in Your Word, I receive salvation now. Thank You for saving me."

The very moment you commit your life to Jesus Christ, the truth of His Word instantly comes to pass in your spirit. Now that you're born again, there's a brand-new you!

Please contact us and let us know that you've prayed to receive Jesus as your Savior. We'd like to send you some free materials to help you on your new journey. Call our Helpline: **719-635-1111** (available 24 hours a day, seven days a week) to speak to a staff member who is here to help you understand and grow in your new relationship with the Lord.

Welcome to your new life!

Receive the Holy Spirit

As His child, your loving heavenly Father wants to give you the supernatural power you need to live a new life. *"For every one that asketh receiveth; and he that seeketh findeth; and to him that knocketh it shall be opened…how much more shall* your *heavenly Father give the Holy Spirit to them that ask him?"* (Luke 11:10–13).

All you have to do is ask, believe, and receive! Pray this: "Father, I recognize my need for Your power to live a new life. Please fill me with Your Holy Spirit. By faith, I receive it right now. Thank You for baptizing me. Holy Spirit, You are welcome in my life."

Some syllables from a language you don't recognize will rise up from your heart to your mouth (1 Cor. 14:14). As you speak them out loud by faith, you're releasing God's power from within and building yourself up in the spirit (1 Cor. 14:4). You can do this whenever and wherever you like.

It doesn't really matter whether you felt anything or not when you prayed to receive the Lord and His Spirit. If you believed in your heart that you received, then God's Word promises you did. *"Therefore I say unto you, What things soever ye desire, when ye pray, believe that ye receive* them, *and ye shall have* them" (Mark 11:24). God always honors His Word—believe it!

We would like to rejoice with you, pray with you, and answer any questions to help you understand more fully what has taken place in your life!

Please contact us to let us know that you've prayed to be filled with the Holy Spirit and to request the book *The New You & the Holy Spirit*. This book will explain in more detail about the benefits of being filled with the Holy Spirit and speaking in tongues. Call our Helpline: **719-635-1111** (available 24 hours a day, seven days a week).

Call for Prayer

If you need prayer for any reason, you can call our Helpline, 24 hours a day, seven days a week at **719-635-1111**. A trained prayer minister will answer your call and pray with you.

Every day, we receive testimonies of healings and other miracles from our Helpline, and we are ministering God's nearly-too-good-to-be-true message of the Gospel to more people than ever. So, I encourage you to call today!

About the Author

Andrew Wommack's life was forever changed the moment he encountered the supernatural love of God on March 23, 1968. As a renowned Bible teacher and author, Andrew has made it his mission to change the way the world sees God.

Andrew's vision is to go as far and deep with the Gospel as possible. His message goes far through the *Gospel Truth* television program, which is available to over half the world's population. The message goes deep through discipleship at Charis Bible College, headquartered in Woodland Park, Colorado. Founded in 1994, Charis has campuses across the United States and around the globe.

Andrew also has an extensive library of teaching materials in print, audio, and video. More than 200,000 hours of free teachings can be accessed at **awmi.net**.

Contact Information

Andrew Wommack Ministries, Inc.

PO Box 3333
Colorado Springs, CO 80934-3333
info@awmi.net
awmi.net

Helpline: 719-635-1111 (available 24/7)

Charis Bible College

info@charisbiblecollege.org
844-360-9577
CharisBibleCollege.org

For a complete list of all of our offices,
visit **awmi.net/contact-us**.

Connect with us on social media.

Sign up to watch anytime, anywhere, for free.

GOSPEL TRUTH
NETWORK

GTNTV.com

Download our apps available on mobile and TV platforms or stream GTN on Glorystar Satellite Network.

Andrew's
LIVING
COMMENTARY
BIBLE SOFTWARE

Andrew Wommack's *Living Commentary* Bible study software is a user-friendly, downloadable program. It's like reading the Bible with Andrew at your side, sharing his revelation with you verse by verse.

Main features:

- Bible study software with a grace-and-faith perspective
- Over 26,000 notes by Andrew on verses from Genesis through Revelation
- *Matthew Henry's Concise Commentary*
- 11 Bible versions
- 2 concordances: *Englishman's Concordance* and *Strong's Concordance*
- 2 dictionaries: *Collaborative International Dictionary* and *Holman's Dictionary*
- Atlas with biblical maps
- Bible and *Living Commentary* statistics
- Quick navigation, including history of verses
- Robust search capabilities (for the Bible and Andrew's notes)
- "Living" (i.e., constantly updated and expanding)
- Ability to create personal notes

Whether you're new to studying the Bible or a seasoned Bible scholar, you'll gain a deeper revelation of the Word from a grace-and-faith perspective.

Purchase Andrew's *Living Commentary* today at **awmi.net/living**, and grow in the Word with Andrew.

Item code: 8350

ANDREW WOMMACK MINISTRIES

There's more on the website.

Discover **FREE** teachings, testimonies, and more by scanning the QR code or visiting **awmi.net**.

Continue to grow in the Word of God!
You will be blessed!

Your monthly giving make the greatest kingdom impac

When you give, you mak an impact in the kingdo that lasts for generation Your generosity enable our phone ministers t answer calls 24/7. You support is also expandir Charis Bible College ar allowing *The Gospel Tru* to reach an even wide global audience. You d this and more throug your giving each mont

Become a Grace Partner today! Scan the QR code, visit **awmi.net/partr** or call our Helpline at **719-635-1111** and select option five for Partners

God has **more** for you.

Are you longing to find your God-given purpose? At Charis Bible College you will establish a firm foundation in the Word of God and receive hands-on ministry experience to **find, follow,** and **fulfill** your purpose.

Scan the QR code for a free Charis teaching!

CharisBibleCollege.org
Admissions@awmcharis.com
(844) 360-9577

Change your life. **Change the world.**